THE CLASSICAL MOMENT

THE
CLASSICAL
MOMENT

STUDIES OF
CORNEILLE, MOLIÈRE
AND RACINE

BY
MARTIN TURNELL

"I recommend theatrical representations to you, which are excellent at Paris. The tragedies of Corneille and Racine, and the comedies of Molière, well attended to, are admirable lessons, both for the heart and the head. There is not, nor ever was, any theatre comparable to the French"

—Letter from Lord Chesterfield to his Son

GREENWOOD PRESS, PUBLISHERS
WESTPORT, CONNECTICUT

The Library of Congress cataloged this book as follows:

Turnell, Martin.
  The classical moment : studies of Corneille, Molière, and
Racine. Westport, Conn., Greenwood Press ₁1971₁

  xv, 261 p. ports. 23 cm.

  "Originally published in 1948."
  Bibliography : p. 251–257.

  1. Corneille, Pierre, 1606–1684. 2. Molière, Jean Baptiste Poquelin,
1622–1673. 3. Racine, Jean Baptiste, 1639–1699.   I. Title.

PQ527.T8 1971	842'.4'09	79–138601
ISBN 0-8371-5803-6		MARC
Library of Congress	71 ₁4₁	

Originally published in 1948 by New Directions, New York

Reprinted with the permission of New Directions Publishing Corporation

Reprinted in 1975 by Greenwood Press
A division of Congressional Information Service, Inc.,
88 Post Road West, Westport, Connecticut 06881

Library of Congress Catalog Card Number 79-138601

ISBN 0-8371-5803-6

Printed in the United States of America

10 9 8 7 6 5 4

FOR HELEN

PREFACE

"ENGLISHMEN," said Lytton Strachey, "have always loved Molière. It is hardly an exaggeration to say that they have always detested Racine."

It is due very largely to Strachey's two brief studies that Racine now has a certain following among admirers of French literature in this country. The production of *Phèdre* by members of the Comédie Française in London last year was a great step in the right direction, but there is still much to be done before his work is recognized for what it is—one of the summits of European poetry. It would, perhaps, be an exaggeration to say that Englishmen to-day "detest" Racine, but we are still far from the happy state of affairs described by a Belgian observer. In an article written shortly after the liberation of his country, he declared that the English are the most civilized people in the world because English bankers spend their leisure pruning their rose trees and reading Racine. For Racine remains a difficult writer for many English readers, and the author of an article on "Un-English Tastes," which appeared in *The Times Literary Supplement* a year before the war, remarked:

"There are, no doubt, genuine English 'fans' of Racine, though surely not many. But with all the good will in the world and complete faith in the standards of French classicism the rest of us sigh heavily over the resounding syllables of *Andromaque* and *Bérénice* and prefer to think of *Antony and Cleopatra*. Racine, we agree, loses nothing of his stature because we cannot greatly enjoy him; our trouble, perhaps, is that we have not yet so habituated ourselves to values of literature other than our own as to experience the delight he offers."

These difficulties seem to me to be real ones and the attitude of respectful incomprehension much more promising than the arrogant dislike of former generations. It has long been recognized by the French themselves that Racine presents a serious obstacle to foreigners and it is curious to observe that a remark of M. François Mauriac's confirms in its own way the findings of *The Times* critic:

"Of all our authors," he writes, "Racine is one of the least accessible to the peoples of other countries. His realm is that borderland between the head and the heart where no one can penetrate who does not belong to the French family. When a foreigner tells us that he is fond of Racine and recites a few lines in a certain tone of voice, we know that he has nothing left to learn about France."[1]

The writer in *The Times* seems to put his finger on one of the main difficulties when he points out with M. Mauriac that it is precisely because he is so French that Racine is so difficult for foreigners. Now an understanding of Racine means primarily an appreciation of his greatness as a poet. It is, unfortunately, a problem that our French friends can do little to help us solve. They realize like M. Mauriac that Racine is peculiarly "inaccessible," but they cannot help us to overcome difficulties which for them simply do not exist. Popular works on Racine from Jules Lemaître to the admirable M. Pierre Brisson are in the main penetrating psychological studies of Racine's *characters*. They have comparatively little to say about his poetry beyond holding up for our admiration a few lines here and there which to many English readers are no more than "resounding syllables."

There are lines in Racine which are "poetical" by any standards. When he says

Dans l'Orient désert quel devint mon ennui!

huge vistas of desolation unfold before us and the one word, *désert*, welds the desolation of man and the desolation of nature.

He has only to say

C'était pendant l'horreur d'une profonde nuit.

for a bottomless abyss of terror to open before our eyes.

In spite of the "formal" language, a single line conjures up the peace of night and the silence of sleeping armies:

Mais tout dort, et l'armée, et les vents, et Neptune.

or the decadence of an Eastern potentate:

La molle oisiveté des enfants des sultans.

Racine is a master of the single line certainly, but it would be shirking the main difficulty to pretend that the bulk of his poetry is as easy to appreciate as these lines. Although Racine seems to

[1] *Journal*, III, Paris, 1940, p. 203.

present special difficulties, they are only part of a larger difficulty which is well brought out by *The Times* critic in the same article.

"There is no foreign literature," he writes, "to which English taste is so sympathetic as the literature of France; but only a relatively small part of French poetry 'appeals' to the French-speaking Englishman, and even in a great deal of French fiction he discovers a less than sympathetic and sometimes faintly inimical quality."

The movement and style of French poetry and the mind behind it may sometimes appear very different from English, but French poetry is not a special kind of poetry. It can be enjoyed by anyone with a good sensibility and a reasonable knowledge of the language; but in order to enjoy Racine to the full, to attain that "delight" which so tantalizingly eludes *The Times* critic, we are called upon to make a definite mental adjustment. It is a question not of choosing between Shakespeare and Racine, between English and French poetry, but of extending our experience by accustoming ourselves to fresh ways of thinking and feeling, to a new vision. It is not enough to rid ourselves of a number of critical preconceptions; we must realize that poetry which lacks many of the qualities that we have come to think inseparable from all poetry may yet be among the greatest poetry that there is.

The only way to enjoy Racine is to soak oneself in his poetry, to surrender oneself completely to his sensibility. There is no short cut, no convenient text-and-translation. Shakespeare has been translated into French, Molière and much more recent poets into English, and a good deal of these writers has survived in translation; but Racine remains one of the few great masters who is absolutely untranslatable. When you know him, almost every line he wrote, however simple, however commonplace the vocabulary, has a charm and music of its own; but if you try to translate him everything goes. Racine in English dress is practically indistinguishable from the authors of the minor tragedies of the Restoration period.

It has seemed natural in writing of Racine to include in the same book studies of the two other great French dramatists of the seventeenth century—Corneille and Molière. Corneille is in some ways a more difficult poet for Englishmen than Racine because on the surface he appears still less "poetical" and his syllables are, as they are certainly meant to be, "resounding." Moreover, an appreciation of his genius was scarcely helped by the sort of production of his plays that we witnessed in England between the wars until, like Racine, he, too, was tactfully dropped from the repertoire of our distinguished visitors. For those who know and love his work Racine is incomparable and irreplaceable; but it must be admitted that of the three poets discussed here, Molière is far and away the most "accessible." Yet though "Englishmen have always loved Molière," it will hardly be maintained that we are overburdened with good criticism of his work in English or that he is as widely read and enjoyed as he should be. The very fact that he is so "accessible" also helps us to appreciate the contrast with Corneille and Racine and, I hope, to make them more intelligible.

There is another reason for studying the seventeenth century in general and its three greatest dramatists in particular at the present time. After being cut off from France for over four years, Englishmen admire French literature more passionately and await the latest books and periodicals from Paris more eagerly than ever before. While this is an attitude that we must all applaud, there is a reservation to be made. The French tradition is far more homogeneous than our own and the connection between writers belonging to different centuries is far closer than in England. It is difficult to obtain a real insight into French literature or, as M. Mauriac puts it, to become a member of "the French family," if we limit our reading, as we are tempted to do, to the great nineteenth-century writers, who have had a decisive influence on contemporary English literature, and to living authors.

The English critic takes a knowledge of the classics of his own literature for granted; it is an essential part of his critical equipment. Unless he knows Donne he cannot speak with any confidence of Eliot, and the profound linguistic originality of Hopkins can only be grasped by someone who knows Shakespeare. The same thing is true of French literature. We cannot hope to appreciate French poetry to the full, or to the fullest extent of our capacity, if we approach French writers as isolated individuals. We have to soak ourselves in the French tradition until we are almost a part of it. For we can only judge French writers when we find ourselves automatically comparing them with the great French classics. We cannot understand Baudelaire unless we know Racine and are capable of perceiving the force of Gourmont's remark that his poetry is a return to traditional French versification. Unless we know the seventeenth century as well as the eighteenth, we cannot understand what Laclos was attacking in the *Liaisons dangereuses* or why the attack was made, so that without its proper background the book may appear to be no more than a pornographic novel written with uncommon psychological insight and an uncommon sense of style instead of the masterpiece that it undoubtedly is. Unless we know the seventeenth and eighteenth centuries, we shall undoubtedly miss much that Constant and Stendhal have to offer. Flaubert is naturally one of the key-figures in the development of the modern novel; we cannot appreciate Henry James and Conrad in England or Proust in France without understanding his peculiar technical accomplishment. We must go further than this and say that it is difficult to appreciate either the undeniable originality of Flaubert himself or his painful weaknesses without a sound knowledge of the classic French novelists and of the atmosphere of Flaubert's formative years. It is only when we realize this that we can begin to form a true picture of the development of European literature and to understand the significance of the great French writers for us as Englishmen.

It is evident that the more we read, the greater will be our enjoyment and the surer our judgment of French literature. I do not pretend that a knowledge of the three writers discussed here or even of the whole of seventeenth-century literature is sufficient; but it does seem to me to be the essential foundation.

It remains to add that none of these studies makes any claim to completeness. I have tried first to give a general account of the three poets in relation to the social and literary background of their age, then to illustrate what seem to me to be the essential qualities of their poetry by a closer examination of the texts of some of their greatest works. If I have done something to encourage English readers to study them more carefully and with greater pleasure and, above all, to help them to enjoy stage productions of their work when the opportunity occurs, my labour will have been well repaid.

I have to thank my friends Professor P. Mansell Jones and Miss Sonia Brownell for their kindness in reading the proofs and for making a number of valuable suggestions.

Parts of this book have appeared in somewhat different form in *Horizon* and *Scrutiny* and I am indebted to the Editors of those journals for permission to reproduce them here. Acknowledgments are also due to Messrs. G. Bell & Sons, Ltd. for allowing me to quote from Mr. John Palmer's *Molière: His Life and Works,* and to Mr. W. Somerset Maugham and Messrs. William Heinemann, Ltd. for *The Summing Up.*

August, 1946   M.T.

CONTENTS

LIST OF ILLUSTRATIONS

THE
SEVENTEENTH CENTURY

1

T H E seventeenth century in England and France was one of the greatest ages in European civilization. We are inclined in England to take the *grand siècle* too much for granted, to treat it as a text-book phrase without appreciating the reality for which it stands or the splendour of its achievement. The literature of the country which produced Corneille, Molière, Racine, La Fontaine, Bossuet, Pascal, Fénelon, Descartes, La Bruyère, La Rochefoucauld, Saint-Simon, Saint-Évremond, Madame de La Fayette and Madame de Sévigné was certainly not inferior to that of any other European country. France had no Shakespeare, but between 1600 and 1700 she probably produced more great writers than England, and their range and variety were in some respects wider. The greatest of the English writers were nearly all poets. England had no religious writers of the stature of Bossuet and the depth of Pascal, no moralists and memoir-writers who were the equals of La Rochefoucauld, La Bruyère or Saint-Simon, no novelist who wrote anything which is so obviously a "classic" as the *Princesse de Clèves*. Saint-Évremond's literary criticism makes Dryden's sound like the essays of a respectable member of the sixth form; and compared with Descartes Hobbes appears crude and shallow.

In both countries it was an age of violent contrasts, of great successes and resounding failures, of great splendour and appalling squalor; but though the same spirit seems to dominate the whole Continent, French literature makes a very different impression on the mind from English. We shall only understand the reasons for this and learn to appreciate the masterpieces produced in both countries to the full when we know something of the historical background.

The Englishman who approaches the poetry of the *grand siècle* for the first time misses the colour and fantasy, the racy colloquialism and the love of homely detail which are native to the English genius. It was not always so. In the Middle Ages English and French poetry was often very close. Chaucer and Villon possessed the same firm grasp of the world of external reality and the same power of placing things vividly before our eyes. It was because they had their roots deep in the common life of their time and spoke for the community as an undivided whole that we are more conscious of their resemblances than their differences, that they are far closer to one another than Racine is to Shakespeare.

The close of the Middle Ages, the disruption of Christendom and the rise of the nation-state split Europe in two. They mark a parting of the ways for the cultures of the Northern and the Mediterranean peoples in general, and of England and France in particular. The Mediterranean peoples retired behind the Pyrenees and the Alps, the English to their island, only emerging to do battle with one another in an attempt to impose their own systems on their rivals. Germany was in a state of chaos and, in spite of her geographical position, France suffered from the same disadvantages as her neighbours.

The effect of this cleavage on European art was immense. English poetry retained its native vigour, and the primitive folk-element which was present in all medieval art, until the latter part of the century; but in France poetry became more and more the expression of a civilized *élite*. The emphasis falls on decorum, on the virtues of clarity and order, and there is a growing horror among French writers of "Gothic barbarism":

> Cette grande roideur des vertus des vieux âges
> Heurte trop notre siècle et les communs usages.

It is not difficult to see why this was so. In England, the country where the Reformation triumphed, the people were united in their opposition to Spain. The merchant-adventurers, who were also the men who defeated the Armada, contributed to the unity and Shakespeare's "rabble" were the "other ranks" who manned their vessels in the same struggle. In France, the country where the Reformation was signally defeated, the unity was much less broadly based and far more precarious; it was the unity of throne and nobility; and while English culture remained in many ways a popular one, French came to depend more and more on the aristocratic idea. Neither country was directly affected by the Counter-Reformation and there was practically no Baroque art. (Eighteenth-century Rococo was a different matter.) England, however, was less isolated culturally as she was less isolated politically. The influence of the Italian and Spanish schools of poetry was introduced by scholars and travellers like Donne and a Catholic convert like Crashaw; but the innovations were assimilated by the English genius which for the next two hundred years set its face steadfastly against the Latin virtues.[1] France was preoccupied with the problems of internal and external security and concentrated on the development of her natural virtues to the virtual exclusion of foreign elements. The tendency to rhetoric, which is inherent in French verse, becomes more pronounced during the seventeenth century and is a sign that the poet is already conscious of the instability of the society in which he is living.[2]

This fundamental cleavage has persisted down to our own times. In the nineteenth century English readers found the French romantic poets and, much later, Verlaine, more to their taste than the seventeenth-century masters; but it is only during the present century that there has been a genuine *rapprochement*. In many ways the poetry of the School of Baudelaire is closer to the Metaphysical Poets than to other kinds of English or French poetry written in the nineteenth century. It is the bridge between the Metaphysical Poets and contemporary English and French poetry and, indeed, between English and French poetry as a whole. The intellectual as well as the territorial frontiers, one feels, have been abolished. There is a common *malaise* and a common use of imagery drawn from industrial civilization and from experimental psychology.

It is, however, with the seventeenth century that I am mainly concerned here, and the differences between English and French poetry will be more readily apparent if we compare a few lines from Donne's *Calme* with the description of the calm in Racine's *Iphigénie*:

> As steady' as I can wish, that my thoughts were,
> Smooth as thy mistresse glasse or what shines there,
> The sea is now. And, as the Iles which wee
> Seeke, when wee can move, our ships rooted bee.
> As water did in stormes, now pitch runs out:
> As lead, when a fir'd Church becomes one spout.

[1] V. Praz, *Secentismo e Marinismo in Inghilterra*, Florence, 1925.

[2] There were Spanish and Italian influences in Corneille and Molière, but they were not of the kind or extent which invalidates the general thesis maintained here.

And all our beauty, and our trimme, decayes,
Like courts removing, or like ended playes.
The fighting place now seamens ragges supply;
And all the tackling is a frippery.

.   .   .

Tu te souviens du jour qu'en Aulide assemblés,
Nos vaisseaux par les vents semblaient être appelés.
Nous partions; et déjà, par mille cris de joie,
Nous menacions de loin les rivages de Troie.
Un prodige étonnant fit taire ce transport:
Le vent, qui nous flattait, nous laissa dans le port.
Il fallut s'arrêter, et la rame inutile
Fatigua vainement une mer immobile.

The first thing which strikes us is that Donne builds up his picture
by accumulating a great number of significant details which place
the *physical* scene compellingly before our eyes. The ships are
"rooted" like the islands for which they are making, and later in
the poem they become our "bed-ridde ships." The molten pitch
pours out in the sweltering heat whose fiery blast strikes at us from
the printed page. The next thing we notice is that the lines are at
once popular and colloquial and extremely erudite. In the terse
reference to the lead streaming out of a "fir'd Church" which has
become a single "spout" of flame, the poet is a spectator, is "one
of the people," mingling with the sweaty London crowd which
gazes idly, helplessly with open mouth at the fire. The ship's
tackle, once so elegant, "decayes" and becomes a "frippery,"
reminding him—for he is an aristocrat as well as a man of the
people—of the tawdry stage properties left behind when the court
removes or the play comes to an end.

There is nothing comparable to this, you may feel, in Racine's
lines; but his aim is very different from Donne's. It is no part
of his intention to paint a vivid picture of the physical appearance
of the scene or to amuse his audience with the quaint and erudite
reflections that pass through the mind of a cultivated man who is
stranded on the high seas as Donne does in

Onely the Calenture together drawes
Deare friends, which meet dead in great fishes jawes:
And on the hatches as on Altars lyes
Each one, his owne Priest, and owne Sacrifice.

Racine's interest is concentrated on the drama that is going on inside the character's mind, on the contrast between the excited warriors anxious to "get at" the Trojans—

> . . . par mille cris de joie,
> Nous menacions de loin les rivages de Troie.

—and the sense of hopeless frustration caused by the calm. The commonplace, colourless little words do somehow contrive to suggest the great fleet eager like the crews to join battle:

> Nos vaisseaux par les vents semblaient être appelés.

Then the calm descends in all its suddenness:

> Le vent, qui nous flattait, nous laissa dans le port.

The *flattait* is a characteristic example of Racine's elegance. In the final couplet the tension reaches its last extreme. The skilful mingling of the r's and m's and the liquid l's makes us feel the oars beating helplessly against the heavy, motionless waters; but the emphasis falls on *fatigua*, on the sense of complete and hopeless frustration.

I think that we can go on to describe the principal difference between the literatures of the two countries by saying that English literature was a literature of *expansion* and French a literature of concentration and *consolidation*. This statement, however, needs some qualification. In the sixteenth century the literature of both countries was a literature of expansion, but at the end of the century we notice a change in France. It was in the poetry of Malherbe that French literature formally turned its back on the Gothic past and began the process of consolidation which will distinguish it all through the seventeenth century. There was no such change in English literature which was dominated for most of the seventeenth century by a spirit of adventure and discovery, by a determined attempt to extend the whole field of human experience. In his essay on "The Metaphysical Poets," Mr. T. S. Eliot has spoken of "a mechanism of sensibility which could devour any kind of experience." The words describe with felicity the way in which the frontiers of poetry were extended and we see the process at work in a line of Donne's where he addresses his mistress as

> . . . my America! my new-found-land.

The great geographical discoveries of the age are reflected in its poetry and are paralleled by the discoveries which the poets make about the human mind. Their borrowings from the language of philosophy, astronomy, mathematics and the other sciences reveal the effort to map the inner world with the same care and thoroughness with which the great navigators were mapping the outer world, to establish relations between realms of experience which seem at first to have little in common.

This, however, is by no means the whole of the story. We must go on to point out that English poetry in the seventeenth century reflects a state of great emotional turmoil, a sense of unending and, at times, well-nigh intolerable spiritual tension. Its principal figures are almost all *tourmentés*, fighting a relentless and solitary battle against death and doubt. Donne, fretting silently in his room over the ravages of the "new philosophy," is the classic example of what has been well called "the Baroque doubt"; but scarcely one of them escaped from the gentle Herbert, wondering whether he really belonged to Canterbury or Rome, to Milton who wrote a "Christian epic" which betrays in every line his utter disbelief in the fundamental tenets of the Christian system.

The short journey across the Channel introduces us to a world which appears to be as different from ours as it could well be. There are modern French writers who speak to me more urgently, more intimately than any of the seventeenth-century masters, who seem more necessary to me; but I always return to the seventeenth century with a sense of undisguised relief. For here, one feels, is something solid and firm on which the mind can rest; a circumscribed world no doubt, but a world with clearly defined boundaries; a world which speaks with many voices, but on all the major problems of human life each voice proclaims the same message, delivered without the slightest hesitation. French society was highly centralized and very compact, and there is a passage in the *Critique de l'École des femmes* which throws some light on its structure. The speaker, who represents Molière's own views, declares that

"la grande épreuve de toutes vos comédies, c'est le jugement de la Cour; que c'est son goût qu'il faut étudier pour trouver l'art de réussir; qu'il n'y a point de lieu où les décisions soient si justes; et, sans mettre en ligne de compte tous les gens savants qui y sont, que, du simple bon sens naturel et du commerce de tout le beau monde, on s'y fait une manière d'esprit qui, sans comparaison, juge plus finement des choses que tout le savoir enrouillé des pédants."

The keynote of the century is authority and the word which occurs perhaps more frequently than any other is *les règles*. There are rules in religion, in conduct, in art. "There is an immense effort," writes M. Daniel Mornet, "to establish everywhere an order which is as reasonable as the order of mathematics, to organize a sort of social and æsthetic geometry."[1] France was not without her rebels, but it must be emphasized that the authority of "the rules" was not in the main a tyrannical one. The history of authority in the seventeenth century is the history of an authority which was freely accepted because it was felt to be *reasonable*. In art, in particular, the application of the rules was tempered by what Molière calls in the passage I have just quoted the "simple bon sens naturel" and the "commerce de tout le beau monde."[2]

I have already suggested that the movement towards consolidation began in France in the second half of the sixteenth century, and it is worth while examining this point a little more closely. When we turn to French literary criticism in the seventeenth century, we discover that there were two main trends. There were the liberalism of Saint-Évremond and the conservatism of Boileau, and their interaction did much to give the literature of the seventeenth century its geniality and its poise. I do not think that Boileau was a great writer, but, as so often happens, the cross-currents of an age are more apparent and easier to follow in the work of secondary writers than in the work of the masters. In an impressive defence of Sainte-Beuve, Remy de Gourmont said that a critic must be a "creator of values"; and he went on to show that in the seventeenth century Boileau had determined or "created" the values of the French poets of the Middle Ages and that his "placing" of them had lasted for two hundred years.[3] There is no doubt that Boileau's influence was immense and his career is very instructive

[1] *Histoire de la littérature et de la pensée françaises*, Paris, 1927, p. 75.

[2] The foundation of the French Academy in 1635 was at bottom an expression of a felt need for a central authority, but once founded the Academy tended to foster repressive tendencies.

[3] "Sainte-Beuve Créateur de Valeurs" in *Promenades philosophiques*, I, Paris, 1913.

for anyone who wishes to understand the seventeenth century. He was not, perhaps, a particularly original thinker, but he was undoubtedly the spokesman of his age or more precisely of its conservative tendencies which he proceeded to express in remarkably lucid and logical form. The influence which Gourmont rightly attributed to him was exercised not by a large work in many volumes, but by a few lines of his *Art poétique.* When he wrote:

> Durant les premiers ans du Parnasse Français,
> Le caprice tout seul faisait toutes les lois.
> La Rime, au bout des mots assemblés sans mesure,
> Tenait lieu d'ornements, de nombre et de césure.
> Villon sut le premier, dans ces siècles grossiers,
> Débrouiller l'art confus de nos vieux Romanciers.

he succeeded in branding almost all French poetry down to the end of the sixteenth century as clumsy and incomprehensible, and in reducing Villon to a talented barbarian who might have done quite creditably in a more propitious age. His propaganda was so effective that living French critics are still busily engaged in removing the stigma and rediscovering the sixteenth century.[1]

The shortcomings of Boileau's approach are fully apparent when, a few lines later in the same passage, he remarks:

> Ronsard qui le suivit, par une autre méthode
> Réglant tout, brouilla tout, fit un art à sa mode:
> Et toutefois longtemps eut un heureux destin.
> Mais sa Muse en Français parlant Grec et Latin,
> Vit dans l'âge suivant par un retour grotesque,
> Tomber de ses grands mots le faste pédantesque.

The crux of this passage is not the slighting reference to Ronsard's achievement, but the line

> Mais sa Muse en Français parlant Grec et Latin . . .

For it was precisely the linguistic experiments of the sixteenth-century poets and their power of assimilating words from other languages which were the signs of their immense vitality, of their tendency towards expansion which Boileau and Malherbe before him were so eager to curb.

The *Art poétique* also contains a vigorous statement of Boileau's

[1] V. Thierry Maulnier. *Introduction à la poésie française,* Paris, 1939.

positive values, is indeed a veritable breviary of the *mots d'ordre*
of the seventeenth century:

> Quelque sujet qu'on traite, ou plaisant, ou sublime,
> Que toujours le Bon sens s'accorde avec la Rime.
>
> Aimez donc la Raison. Que toujours vos écrits
> Empruntent d'elle seule et leur lustre et leur prix.
>
> Tout doit tendre au Bon sens: mais pour y parvenir
> Le chemin est glissant et pénible à tenir.
> Pour peu qu'on s'en écarte, aussitôt l'on se noie.
> La Raison, pour marcher, n'a souvent qu'une voie.

It was, however, in the famous eulogy of Malherbe that Boileau's
talent proved most effective and, in view of the subsequent history
of French literary taste, I think we must add most dangerous:

> Enfin Malherbe vint, et le premier en France,
> Fit sentir dans les vers une juste cadence:
> D'un mot mis en sa place enseigna le pouvoir,
> Et réduisit la Muse aux règles du devoir.
> Par ce sage Écrivain la Langue réparée
> N'offrit plus rien de rude à l'oreille épurée.
> Les Stances avec grâce apprirent à tomber,
> Et le vers sur le vers n'osa plus enjamber.
> Tout reconnut ses lois, et ce guide fidèle
> Aux auteurs de ce temps sert encor de modèle.

In a sense the whole of the seventeenth century is there with its
air of authority and its finality, its *Bon sens, juste cadence, règles du
devoir*, its *grâce*, its *pureté* and its *clarté*. The whole of the seventeenth
century, we may add, except its inspiration and its incomparable
sensibility.

It is time now to pursue our investigation in a somewhat different
field.

> Le bon sens est la chose du monde la mieux partagée . . .

The opening words of the *Discours de la méthode*, with their
confidence and their obvious reasonableness, emphasize one of the
basic values of the *grand siècle*, and the way in which they rein-
force the tenets of the *Art poétique* demonstrates the remarkable
unity of thought in that age. It is no doubt true that the work

B*

of Descartes spelt the ruin of traditional philosophy, marking the change from a philosophy of *being* to a philosophy of *knowing;* but on the fundamental values of civilization Descartes himself was completely intransigent, and so far from undermining them, his aim was to justify and strengthen them and to provide them with a philosophical basis. He was at pains to prove at every step that his "method" was a reasonable one, and when he overthrew the authority of Aristotle, he did so in the name of *bon sens* and at once proceeded to set up in its place a new authority which was not less solid.

It is the existence of authority that gives the literature its external order and its internal tension. Descartes and Boileau speak naturally of *bon sens, raison* and *nature,* but these were only some of the terms which express the "basic verities" of seventeenth-century civilization and which recur in all its writings. Others are *ordre, mesure, équité, bon goût, justesse, bornes,* and *esprit.* A critic like Boileau was constantly trying to determine their place in poetry, while a moralist like La Bruyère tried to determine their correct relations to one another or, to put it in another way, to consolidate the essential human values. When he writes

"Talent, goût, esprit, bon sens, choses différentes, non incompatibles.
"Entre le bon sens et le bon goût il y a la différence de la cause à un effet.
"Entre esprit et talent il y a la proportion du tout à sa partie"

—we know that this is the voice of a man living in a world in which it is natural to speak of measure and proportion. The whole tendency of the century was to express itself in brief, pithy maxims.

We find the same tendency at work in definitions like the *honnête homme,* the *belle âme* and the *grand cœur.* We shall never appreciate the literature of the age to the full until we realize that these terms are in no sense abstractions, but stand for something as vivid and real as the life which pulsates in the words *amour, passion, gloire* and *honneur* which enshrine values of a different kind. Descartes' preoccupation with *idées claires et distinctes* is symptomatic. The only things, he said, of which we can be sure are those of which we have clear and distinct ideas, and that describes the whole policy of the century. The policy can be defined as the conquest of experience. There was an unceasing effort to translate more and more of human experience into formulas, to reclaim it from the vast hinterland which lay just beyond "reason" and "good sense." For as soon as this was achieved, the field of human experience was automatically extended; fresh territories had been brought under the dominion of "reason," more pointers were available to help people to live a "reasonable" life, and the danger of going off the rails and plunging into anarchy was correspondingly diminished.

This process was certainly very different from the one that was going on in England. The English poets were extremely conscious that they were living in a dangerous and perplexing situation, that they were constantly up against the Unknown and that at any moment someone might make a fresh discovery which would shatter their conception of the world. There was, as we shall see, plenty of tension in some of the French writers; but it was in the main tension within a stable world or a world which appeared to be stable, and they were free from the radical uncertainty of the Englishmen. Their work was not a voyage of discovery into the Unknown; it was a minute exploration of a known reality which can best be described as an *approfondissement* of everyday experience. The literary forms chosen by poets and prose-writers—the alexandrine, the maxim and the character—were used both as an intellectual discipline and to present complex material in the most lucid and orderly manner possible; and it is largely the skill with which they handled their medium that gives much of their work an air of disarming simplicity and sometimes made their discoveries appear superficial.

The price that they paid for their achievement was a substantial, but not an exorbitant, one. Their conception of life was limited but it is easy to exaggerate its limitations, as I suspect that M. Daniel Mornet does in the excellent manual to which I have already referred. He tells us that discussion of political, religious and social problems was to all intents and purposes banned and that in social life fantasy and independence were excluded. It is true that "self-expression," as we understand it, was not exactly encouraged, and it may be true that when La Bruyère came to write the *Caractères* he found no rebels in the grand manner and had to confine himself to the *tics* and *manies* of a few eccentrics. It must be remembered, however, that he was not composing a psychological treatise in the manner of Descartes' *Traité des passions de l'âme*, but a work of art. His book is less valuable for its psychological *aperçus* than for a particular kind of wisdom which informs it and transcends the simple phrases. His habit of looking at everything, however trivial it may appear, from the standpoint of unchanging principles produces flashes of insight which illuminate the human scene in a way that is peculiar to the age. When he writes

C'est une grande difformité dans la nature qu'un vieillard amoureux,

we see the amorous old man for the first time and realize why he is shocking and ridiculous.

When M. Mornet goes on to say that the seventeenth century "had no sense of history, no sense of the instability and transitory nature of human societies and of a great number of human rules," he seems to me to give a misleading impression.[1] It is characteristic of the people of the classical ages that they believed very firmly in their own time, believed that they had achieved such a high degree of civilization that the future could only lead to decline. Now there seems to me to have been far more change and development in seventeenth-century France than is commonly allowed, and it is almost certainly the perfection of its literary forms and the regularity with which human experience was "reclaimed" that have obscured the process and produced the impression of a static civilization. Some of the writers were conscious of the uncertainty of the future, and the sense that civilization was disintegrating beneath the polished surface is reflected in individual writers like Racine and Saint-Simon; but it was of the essence of their achievement that this did not undermine their belief in the fundamental sanity of the *universe*. One cannot help being aware in *Athalie* of the doom which is hanging over civilization; but there is also the impression that if the whole Kingdom collapsed and disappeared overnight, Reason, Order and Nature would survive untouched. This is the basic difference between the English and French writers of the seventeenth century. It was not for themselves or their society that the English writers feared; they were the victims of an *angoisse métaphysique* which led them to doubt the ultimate sanity and reasonableness of the universe and which made the French confidence unthinkable for them.

[1] *op. cit.*, p. 76.

2

It is worth glancing next at the subject-matter of seventeenth-century literature:

"About the year 1548," writes M. Georges Duhamel, "France decided to embark on a great work and to spend centuries on it. All Frenchmen who have been associated with it, have been conscious of their part in the great undertaking and have accepted the high degree of discipline which was necessary for so majestic a task.

"What was this work that was undertaken by a whole people? What is this monument which French literature set out to build? The reply can be given at once. It is a portrait of Man.

"French literature has worked untiringly at its task which is nothing less than a full-length portrait of man: the Individual man and the Social man, the Inner and the Outer man, the Visible and the Invisible man, the Subjective and the Objective man."[1]

These words have much to tell us about French literature and the French language. They explain the continuity of French literature from the middle of the sixteenth century down to our own time and the French love of tradition. The great undertaking was undoubtedly helped by the nature of the French language, but here the influence of subject and instrument is a reciprocal one. The French language is singularly well adapted to psychological analysis; but it is also true that the preoccupation with man and his nature has helped to mould language, to make it more the language of the intelligence than the emotions.

It is clear that the great work must, as M. Duhamel points out, last for centuries, must indeed last as long as there are writers. For though man's nature is finite, there is room for change and development; and it thus happens that in each age the accent falls in a different place. Some ages have stressed the Social, others the Individual man; some the Objective, others the Subjective man; but it is because they have all accepted certain fundamental assumptions about human nature that the work of writers as different as Montaigne, Saint-Simon and Proust is clearly part of the task described by M. Duhamel.

[1] *Défense des lettres*, Paris, 1936, pp. 280–1.

"La passion," wrote Pascal in what must have been an unguarded moment,

"La passion ne peut être belle sans excès. Quand on n'aime pas trop, on n'aime pas assez."[1]

In these sentences Pascal puts his finger on the great problem of the seventeenth century. The side of human nature on which they chose to concentrate was precisely the conflict between reason and passion or what Pascal himself, in a more solemn mood, called the "guerre intestine de l'homme entre la raison et les passions."

"This internal war of reason against the passions," he goes on, "has divided those who desire peace into two sects. The first would like to renounce their passions, and become gods; the others would like to renounce reason, and become brute beasts (Des Barreaux). But neither can do as they wish, and reason still remains to condemn the vileness and injustice of the passions and to trouble the repose of those who abandon themselves to them; and the passions always remain alive in those who try to get rid of them."

The dilemma is plain. Whether one liked it or not—many of the seventeenth-century writers emphatically did not—man is endowed with "reason" and "passion" which are in a state of perpetual conflict. "Reason" is constantly trying to bring more and more of human nature under its dominion; "passion" is continually trying to upset the balance and to drive man to the edge of the abyss, to the *espaces infinis* whose silence was a source of fear to Pascal and his contemporaries. Perfect equilibrium was impossible and would indeed be contrary to nature. "For," wrote Pascal in another chapter of the *Pensées*,

"Nothing is so insufferable to man as to be completely at rest, without passions, without business, without distraction, without study. He then becomes aware of his utter nothingness, his forlorness, his insufficiency, his dependence, his weakness, his emptiness. There arise immediately from the depths of his heart feelings of weariness, gloom, sadness, fretfulness, vexation, despair."

The message of these passages is clear. Neither "reason" nor "passion" alone is sufficient to produce "the good life." A man who

---

[1] In the *Discours des passions de l'amour*. It should be observed that in the quotations from the *Pensées* which follow, Pascal does not limit the word "passion" to love; he uses it in the general sense of emotion.

is at the mercy of his passions falls into anarchy, but the man who eliminates or tries to eliminate them altogether is condemned to sterility. A perfect balance between the two is equally unacceptable as a solution because it produces the *plein repos* which opens the door to "weariness, gloom, sadness, fretfulness, vexation" and finally to "despair," which bring him by a different but not less certain route to the abyss. The only healthy condition is a regulated tug-of-war. The peculiar vitality of French literature in the seventeenth century lies in a very delicate poise between "reason" and "passion," in a sense of tension-and-repose which is quite different from the tension of the English writers and which is the result of an ambivalent attitude towards authority. Authority is not accepted passively. It is accepted-and-resisted, and it is this that gives the literature its life, its high degree of emotional vitality combined with a high degree of order.

The regulated tug-of-war is the real theme of the great imaginative writers of the age, of Corneille, Molière, Racine and Madame de La Fayette. It is in no sense an artificial conflict. For, said Jacques Rivière, in the French analysis of human nature "morality itself becomes a psychological element."[1] It is not, save in the case of Pascal, an *angoisse métaphysique*. The writers are haunted by fear of a concrete threat to society, by the fear that it may suddenly be swept away by the excesses of passion; and it was because Racine seemed to his contemporaries, as indeed he was, a reckless champion of the primacy of passion that his work caused such a scandal. There are two short passages at the beginning of the *Princesse de Clèves* which provide a particularly instructive example of the seventeenth-century approach to the subject:

"La magnificence et la galanterie n'ont jamais paru en France avec tant d'éclat que dans les dernières années du règne de Henri second . . . Jamais Cour n'a eu tant de belles personnes et d'hommes admirablement bien faits; et il semblait que la nature eût pris plaisir à placer ce qu'elle donne de plus beau dans les plus grandes princesses et dans les plus grands princes."

"L'ambition et la galanterie étaient l'âme de cette Cour et occupaient également les hommes et les femmes. Il y avait tant d'intérêts et tant de

---

[1] *Le Français*, Paris, 1928, p. 27.

cabales différentes, et les dames y avaient tant de part, que l'amour était toujours mêlé aux affaires, et les affaires à l'amour. Personne n'était tranquille ni indifférent: on songeait à s'élever, à plaire, à servir, ou à nuire; on ne connaissait ni l'ennui ni l'oisiveté, et on était toujours occupé des plaisirs ou des intrigues."

The contrast between the calm, measured movement of the first passage and the breathless, feverish movement of the second shows that the issue was essentially a living one and how deeply the danger was felt.

There is another passage in the same novel which is worth looking at:

"Je lui dis que tant que son affliction avait eu des bornes, je l'avais approuvée et que j'y étais entré; mais que je ne le plaindrais plus s'il s'abandonnait au désespoir et s'il perdait la raison."

This passage is a dramatic statement or, more precisely, an enactment of the seventeenth-century doctrine. Passion cannot be excluded, but it is only permissible so long as it is kept within decent limits, is kept in subjection. Whatever the provocation, the "limits" are absolute; once they are exceeded everything goes.

In a brilliant study of the *Princesse de Clèves*, M. Albert Camus has called the style of the classic writer *une sorte de monotonie passionnée*.[1] It would be difficult to discover words which better describe the effort of the seventeenth-century writers to impose a proper discipline on the emotions that they express, to regulate them by style. This emerges very clearly at the end of *Bajazet* when Osmin announces the death of her lover to Atalide:

> Bajazet est sans vie:
> L'ignoriez-vous?

The studied casualness of the tone in which the momentous announcement is made provokes a violent shock and, at the same time, controls it.

In that very remarkable letter in the *Liaisons dangereuses* in which Madame de Merteuil gives some account of her moral education, she remarks:

[1] In *Problèmes du roman*, Brussels, 1945, p. 193.

"J'étudiai nos mœurs dans les Romans; nos opinions dans les Philosophes; je cherchai même dans les Moralistes les plus sévères ce qu'ils exigeaient de nous, et je m'assurai ainsi de ce qu'on pouvait faire, de ce qu'on devait penser, et de ce qu'il fallait paraître."

This passage brings home very clearly to us the sense in which the great French writers are a living force, are an *école de vie* as well as an *école d'art*. Thought and emotion do not stand still. We have learnt a great deal about human nature since the seventeenth century; considerable progress has been made with the "great work" described by M. Duhamel; but the literature of the seventeenth century as a whole remains a contribution of singular veracity and power to the collective undertaking of all French writers which Stendhal once declared was "the study of the human heart." ·

"There exists outside Rousseau," wrote Jacques Rivière in a passage which only yields its full savour when it is read in French,

"Il existe quelque chose, en dehors de Rousseau, de fort, de puissant, de juste, d'imperturbable, d'impitoyable, une manière directe, stricte et réservée de voir les sentiments, un instinct positif, une lucidité sans phrases, une aptitude à se passer d'appuis et de consolations en face du chaos de l'âme humaine, une délimitation immédiate de ce qui s'y offre de connaissable, qui sont des vertus proprement françaises, et qui ont amené des résultats, aussi bien au point de vue psychologique qu' esthétique, dont on ne soulignera jamais assez l'irremplaçable importance."[1]

These are the virtues which we shall discover in the three great writers whose work is studied in the pages that follow.

[1] *Moralisme et littérature*, Paris, 1932, p 66.

"THE GREAT
AND GOOD CORNEILLE"

1

IT is Corneille's misfortune that no English writer has done for him what Lytton Strachey did for Racine. Whatever the short-comings of Strachey's criticism, it did much to dispose of academic prejudice and to present Racine as a *poet*. It is true that Corneille has never aroused the same antipathy as Racine once did and that he has his place among the immortals on the Albert Memorial; but it is also true that he has never enjoyed the relative popularity which came to Racine with the publication of Strachey's essays. The insistence of living critics that Racine is not merely a great poet, but a great *contemporary* poet, has brought him closer to us, while the figure of Corneille has receded farther and farther into the past. For many of us he has become a sort of historical monu-ment, the lonely representative of a vanished civilization. His poetry suggests Versailles with its vast porticoes and the rigid stone figures hiding coyly among the *bosquets* of its trim gardens or, more formidable still, a scratch troupe from the Comédie Française dressed in those strange, those impossible accoutrements which seem inseparable from the performance of high tragedy, declaiming the *Cid* to an audience of schoolgirls armed with the Hachette plain text. It is ironical to think that the veteran Rodrigue, a little hoarse of voice, a little "gone in the knees," who rants and stamps through five acts for the edification of the School Certificate class, should have become the symbol of the great writer who was all his life the champion of youth in revolt against the corruption and pretence of an older generation.[1]

It is perhaps reassuring to find that this impression is not due entirely to insular prejudice and that Corneille's own country-men have experienced similar difficulties. The most striking thing about the distinguished French critics of the last century is their profound dislike for the great masters of their own literature. Of

[1] It must be added in fairness that these criticisms only apply to the sort of productions we used to see before the "reform" of the Comédie Française towards the end of the 'thirties.